I0529979

DOCTOR/A DE AMOR MADURA Y REBELDE

DOCTOR OF AMBITIOUS & MELANCHOLIC ROMANCE

DAXSON PUBLISHING

Doctor/a de Amor Madura y Rebelde / Doctor of Ambitious and Melancholic Romance
©2025, Alondra Rivera
ISBN: 978-1-966337-10-2
Library of Congress Control Number:

First Edition, 2025

All rights reserved. No part of this publication may be reproduced, distributed,
or transmitted in any for or by any means, including photocopying, recording,
or other electronic or mechanical methods, without the prior written permission
of the publisher, except in the case of brief quotations embodied in critical reviews
and certain other noncommercial uses permitted by copyright law.

Printed in the United States of America

Edited by: DARA, Leslie Manes, Jess Saravia, Milo Santamaria, Ruby Rose
Cover Design by: Jim Dodson and May
Layout Design by: Alondra Rivera

DAXSON PUBLISHING

Dedication

To the love of my life,

wherever you are and wherever you may be

If this book is too much for you then you are not the one for me…

To mis amigos y mi querida familia
My baby girl Stella,
May you grow up to make all the changes
the generations before you
failed to deliver on.
Bring us to a new era of humanity
full of the love and light that was used to create

YOU

Doctor/a de Amor
Madura y Rebelde

Doctor of Ambitious &
Melancholic Romance

Special Shout Outs

My Person (Jamie Rose), thank you for being my #1 best friend, and 1st reader of the earliest drafts of my manuscript... you already know ILYSM

The homies from CLI and RUPO, thank you for saving me from rock bottom. Your art affirmed aspects of myself that I often concealed to blend into professional culture, which was not a natural fit for me. Muchisimas gracias for the lessons that kept me grounded and helped me grow in my artistry.

Special thank you to May/Aiden for the art they shared with me over the year I've known them (including several tattoos). They sketched out the cover art of this book just from rambom images I sent over. Thank you for seeing my chaotic vision and turning it into something beautiful.

To all my past and present teachers, mentors, and professors, especially the ones that failed me—thank you. Your presence in my life taught me lessons no book nor syllabus could have ever prepared me for; cementing my role as a life-long learner.

Mi querida isla "Puerto Rico,"
te amo y te extrañare siempre.

Por favor proteja mi gente, mis queridos animales, y la cultura Boricua
que al fin está en "el spot light".

Muchísimas gracias a todxs lxs artistxs (músicos, autores, poetas, psicólogos, ingenieros, veteranos, estudiantes, curanderxs, brujas, etc) y especialmente a los seres latines que me inspiran todos los días.

My other homes:
Orlando, FL and Pomona, CA— you hold a special place in my heart.

UCF and WesternU of Health Sciences will always be
a haven for me, regardless of time and cultural shifts.

I have left horcruxes in your

libraries, coffee shops, and lecture halls

that you can never break.

TABLE OF CONTENTS

SUBJECTIVE

ASSESSMENT

FOREWORD

Alondra Rivera, BS, DVM (she/they):
A monologue on Writing for those that inspire me to do it

I liken this experience to Anne Frank writing in her diary and F. Kafka in theirs.

These were my greatest [literary/historical] inspirations when I began to compose this manuscript. And more impactful were the real poets I met through poetry class and stumbling through different open mics in the IE... But the trauma I kept hidden in ink-saturated (and tear stained) journals over the years helped me to finish it...

Thank you for those experiences that helped me see the world in black & white, then in technicolor again.

Y a mi familia, los amo tanto.
Espero que este regalito hecho con mucho amor y angustia te llene el alma. Por favor, quiéreme y cuídame, pero no se preocupen por mí que estoy bastante bien.

Writing is therapeutic. Writing is healing. Escribiendo es mi terapia. Escribir me sana.

Writing can be an escape—but mostly, it is freeing. Words decorated in ink on paper; they provide an expansive platform for self-expression... One that I cannot accurately convey with paint on canvas nor with music on a page.

Words: each one more impactful than the last, but together, they tell a story; multiple even, some that may even be foreign to me until they are shared with others who are familiar with these mirrored experiences

Experiences laced with elation / heartbreak / success / failure / isolation / gratitude—

Ultimately, writing is an exploration of self.

The end product is trivial.

This isn't the end for me; the process is what I paid for.

POVMR (Problem Oriented Veterinary Medical Record)

Problem = Pathologizing Poetry

The following works of art are simply that— Arté

And as much as I tried

I simply could not remove

the artist from the work.

These poetic narratives highlight

moments of life

Equally beautiful and painful.

Through "*art therapy*,"

I have found the confidence and capacity

To share them in a unified collection

For your reading pleasure…

Btw… "assume is a compound word"

Ass//u+me

Alondrita, ¿qué quieres?

No llores bebe

Solo dime lo que te sucede

Descansa tus alitas en mis brazos

Tiernos y capaz de aguantar el peso

De tus pensamientos

De tus misterios

De tus miserias

Tranquila, querida amiga—aguanta conmigo

Let your woes melt upon my understanding gaze

Absolve you of all doubt that

Your potential is any less grand than you are

For you are light for those graced by your kindness

Please set me free—help me find my voice—scare away the sadness inside me—
Set me free, please

2024 VETERANS DAY MASHUP

I am an extinct Brown songbird

From the island of Puerto Rico, better known as Borikén

I am a connoisseur of art

But I prefer to hide behind canvas and instruments

Until now — rather recently have I learned the power

Of my voice // my memories

My unique lived-in experience

Which connects me to fellow tortured souls

Mi gente empática, queer, y marginalizada

Latine / Hispanic / mixtos

And the ethnically ambiguous

But especially those that hail from remote Island paradise

Expected to wear the American flag with pride

That flag that no longer resonates with me

You see, I'm the Token Boricua, Morena

That made it out of their hometown.

Born in Mayagüez on the West Coast of PR

Grew up in Universal's backyard and Disney World's playground

Destined to flock to the West Coast of the US

To be the first of their siblings to finish college

And then fucked around and became

The first Doctor in the family

Fucked around and found out what the years of watching Scrubs and Grey's Anatomy was preparing me for.

If you still don't get me:

I'm the token Boricua,

Light skinned Morenita who accepted a seat at

The Western University of Health Science's

College of Veterinary Medicine class of 2022

Only to learn that... I shouldn't love my career so much

Because this is America.

Second year of vet school we were getting bomb threats on campus

Because this is America.

I was trained to take down an active shooter in med school

Because this is America.

A permanent resident of the land of the free,

I get hand-me-down freedom

For the right to choose

To be a lover and a fighter

Breaking ancestral ties with the military—

Broke the cycle of veterans in my family

I became a veterinarian

In Southern California— and yet

I was trained to take down an active shooter in vet school.

Up the street from Downtown Pomona,

I moved into my first home outside of my childhood bedroom,

Found new comforts in the people and spaces around me,

Almost lost myself more times than I can count,

Because this is America.

For a first Gen with the privilege to access higher education—

And you know what?

"Immigrants, we get the job done."

BE STILL AND KNOW

Sunday, November 3, 2024

Dear God,

It has been a while

I have lost faith in you

Maybe I have too much faith

In myself

Because

My heart stands heavy in my chest

Not beating—

 No Beat

Still

 Stillness

Be still and know,

[Well]

I know painfully well what I do not know

And the things I do know

[Well]

They cause me pain too.

And joy— right time and place

With the right company by my side

My heart beats for them

Sincerely,

. . .

UNTITLED

Writer's block and isolation will be the death of me

Every so often // every season

They come for me

Insidious, they trail through the trenches

Open trenches of my mind

Hide behind boundless insecurities and masked behaviors

False smiles exchanged with pleasantries among friends

Reveal those dark thoughts to me alone

When I'm alone they come to the light

The forefront of my mind ablaze with

 Doubt and shame

 That I asked for this

Longed for loneliness

To justify

        The darkness

              Please set me free

How many skins must I shed to

Feel like myself again?

1, 7, 10, 23?

 Skins that were a piece of me

A part of me

Destined to be set free—

Lose all shape and meaning—

Gone from this path

2, 4, 12, 30?

The skins I grew fond of

The skins I hid inside of

The skins I wore for love

3, 9, 18, 26?

Must we shed them wholly

Or flake ourselves away into bits

Slide/slip/saunter out of each limb

Until your core is exposed

And you are left as raw flesh given time

4, 3, 2, 1

A new skin provides the shade I need

Come into the light

  That heavenly glow that bathed you

    Filled your lungs on the first day

    And has guided your voice since

THE PRIVILEGE OF FANS
LOPEZ URBAN FARM, JAN. 8, 2025

There is a special kind of privilege that comes with

Owning a ceiling fan

This year for the first time in years

I had to remind myself to

Wipe down my fans in preparation for the new year

I carefully prepared myself with

A spray bottle

A microfiber towel

A floral scented cleaner

A facemask strapped to my face

With careful precision I carefully swipe away layers of dust

That I hope were only curated by me and my pets over the 8 months I've been renting here

With calculated movements I glide between the blades

      Mindful not to miss the filigree along the margins

Trapping the littlest bit of dust

      Evidence of the neglect I've managed to collect

In the last 8 months...

Absentmindedly I lose a couple dust bunnies and a few tears

Over the memories shared under this fan

Some beautiful

Some haunting

Some almost lost to time

LIFE IS NOT A BEACH

Life is more *like* an elaborately designed maze

Depending on where you got your start

You may be born into a lush oasis

Garden amidst boundless blues and greens
topiaries mesmerizing you at every turn—

Others, less fortunate than you, may be orphaned

Enclosed in a barren landscape

Interrupted by barriers devised of car parts, concrete, and lost dreams

The beach is a haven

For those who were born surrounded by it

We find home in driftwood playgrounds

      Seaweed tangles remind us to mind our feet

The warmth of the sand between our toes while

      Tiny shells and critters hide away from our prints

~~While~~/**And**   The *ocean*/water

It beckons us gently at first

Foamy shores tell us it is safe to venture farther in

Towards the rip tides that threaten to trap us here

For with skill and patience

that only the locals are born with

We evade the threatening throws of waves that could swallow you whole

And instead find comfort in the magnitude of the water

As it holds us steady, between waves and the sun

A gentle reminder to

Simply be

Let the misty air laced with salt and the Moon's promise

To carry your worries away in the water

WHEN HUNGER STRIKES

How do you fight back?
An apple a day is not enough you say?
I challenge you with pizza rolls, taquitos, and empanadillas de carne
Dino shapes nuggets and waffle fries
And if you wanna get fancy Hershey's chocolate pie for desert
Wash it down with an ice-cold Sprite or a(n) _____ Fanta
Because you don't really want water

Don't got time for all of that?

Then maybe a Snicker's bar or a Reese's Cup will do
Yeah right—
 there's that protein bar at the bottom of your bag
You know Mami is waiting for you at home
 Wonder what she'll make today
Spaghetti with meat sauce?
¿Arroz con habichuelas y pollo guisado?
¿Ensalada de papa con bistec encebollado?

Ay las ganas mías—

Forgot I don't live at home anymore
Guess I'll stop for something fast on the way home
Maybe I'll finally return her call too

MELANCHOLIA

The child I will never learn to love   how she haunts my waking hours

With tantrums and trials beyond my capacity

                                testing my tolerance with each bout of hysteria

Taunting my rest with her pervasive presence

                                ever so prominent in the corners of my mind

            She arrests my emotions and

Rearranges   around

            them   around   around

                                around

                                                        the room

Desperate to be acknowledged

            Yearning   to   be   understood

                                I hide her from the world

            Hoard her to my lonely hours

                        Hopeful she does not offend

                        Anyone but me – her maker

            In silence her echoes pervade my world//my mind

            Arresting me to my thoughts/wounds/sorrows

                        You've heard miseria loves company

                                Melancholia demands solitude

Mel-mania, que manía de joderme la vida

GET UNSTUCK

Remove that harsh narrative designed to keep you down

Hide it from your vocabulary so that you can live in the moment

The moment that you have longed to belong to

That present moment you almost lost the right to

That precious moment you earned long ago

Come into the light

       That heavenly glow that bathed you

Filled your lungs on the first day

       And has guided your voice since

                    I've Lost IT / MYSELF / HER

                  Receded into the shell of a human

                  I promised I'd never return to

And what of inspiration?

       Why must she wander away when I need her most?

       Carelessly wandering towards the deep end far from reach

Haunting my dreams with vivid worlds I can never arrive to in the daytime—

Wondrous fantasies lost to the first moments of my waking hour

Until we meet again

LITTLE LOVER GIRL

You see right through me

    Forever in my shadow (to remind me) you

    Are (of) my everlasting light

Rekindle me on my darkest days

For I am unable to ignore the sparkle/glint/dazzle in your

    Eyes when you look (up to) at me

Seeing right through me

    Mirroring the love I thought I'd lost

    Merely hidden away for an opportune time

    Shared with you when my heart allows

    Little Lover Girl,

    My love is yours.

A SNIPPET OF WHAT IT MEANS TO BE A
FIRST/SECOND GEN PRICAN IN THE US OF A

Que es un flamboyan?

Mejor debo preguntar

Como se puede decribrir un flamboyan

Vamos a comenzar

Para los que no saben ni un carajo

Les introduco a la palabra flamboyant— para los que hablan ingles

Y para ayudarlos mas, es un arbol tipico de la isla de PR

{ Y el coqui, por que se llama asi? }

My dad's favorite ENGLISH tagline :

"You got the wrong kind of 'can: I am PuertoRi-CAN, not Mexi-CAN"

Lemme sprinkle in a little context :

EL espa~ol Boricua AKA "Dirty Spanish" according to the Whexican fools I've encountered here in Cali [and their Colombian counterparts//my homies too] sounds as is if Americans made a

"Romance Language   For Dummies"

and it somehow went through a game of telephone, ending up in the not so nice
 Parts of your neighborhood [yeah I mean that ghetto ass street] two blocks over ,
bringing down   the property value of your collection of beige walls surrounded by
concrete, shiplap, and glass   Then marketed as an "excellent starter home for
the modern blue collar family" ...

Bueno,
el Espa~ol Boricua has its charms and is accompanied by a specific type of humor

Lost on those who don't speak Spanish, let alone Spanglish, they would rather
call it non-English

Imaginate // Imagine-ate with me

A language that combines rolling R's with a sexy version of ASL

Pepper in some innuendos that only the real homies will understand

The definitely not PC, NSFW version of the joke your grandfather was too dry to
let slide off his tongue

MIXTAPE FROM THE MIDDLE CHILD

Piss off with the overrated, overdone and outdated rhetoric of

The eldest daughter who

Sacrificed her youth for her siblings

I love you sis but…

You deserved all the consequences sent your way

With that rebellious smile before climbing out of my window to avoid the alarms of the front door

Creeping your way towards empty promises from empty pocketed boys

Boys who still hold pieces of your broken heart

Pieces I've mapped out and turned into stamps

Stamps that I've collected over the years of patience

Patience reserved for the wallflowers silenced to the sidelines of your life

To cheer you on with woodwind instruments wearing outfits

Itchy and stretched-out but also too tight in all the worst places

Gifts from your exhausted closet

Closet full of skeletons you leave front and center

A constant reminder of the niñas you sacrificed for me

Especially when I didn't ask you to

Especially when I hide my own skeletons

       In pieces   littering   corners of my room

          Covered by masking tape   and

Furniture that I love too much to let go

Even though they no longer match the aesthetic

You pre/a/scribed to me many over the years

The aesthetic of: ¿La querida hermana? ¿La niña bonita? Who is that girl?

Oh right the middle child—prim and perfect, living in the shadowed example of her elder sister and gorgeous mother—so generous and thoughtful are they | the ones who refuse to see | the woman she was forced to become | the woman she fought to be | the woman she yearns to hide | for the man who still haunts her dreams | he is only an earshot, a cigarette, a heartbeat away…

PRECISION OF LANGUAGE...

I only forgive you in my dreams

Or rather

I only forgave you in my dreams

       We never had the chance to reconcile things; not in this life—

       At least not yet

As long as we are still alive

There is still a chance

To forgive

And yet

I will

Never

Forget.

REPEAT FIRST LINE 5 TIMES FAST

9/13/2018 8:15pm AMR

I feel like I'm on the verge of a massive panic attack

*

*

*

*

Something feels off like

A premonition of impending doom and

I'm not ready to face it but I am hyper aware of my breathing

Now I can feel my heart beating

In my chest and in my hands

Everyone around me—they feel it too

I see them spilling out the seams, stress becomes each of us

It is starting to sink in

I feel like the oxygen is caught in my throat

Or maybe a well-deserved cry?

*

Am I a big letdown?

*

I don't know how to fix it, but I cannot allow myself to fail

I could never forgive myself. . .

A dense fog—no, a cloud,

of prescribed calm engulfs me

I need to find a way out

END OF APRIL 2023—RENT IS DUE

If you have to FAKE it to make it, then
It isn't worth it FOR either party involved

Rent's due, and I don't have it

In me nor stored away in

A book/ A safe / A mattress

Rent's due

And I have other bills

Threatening me into starvation:

Another month of meatless Mondays

And Tuesdays and Thursdays too

Because I can't afford the end pieces and eggs are priced at a premium

And I'm pretty sure my cat has cancer—

My spirit child, she who came to me born

Amid the fires of Hesperia, became my flame child

With fur the color of flame and charcoal

Rent's due

But so are your hospital bills, plus all the utilities too

And I lost the order on my to-do list

Because I need you

To be comfortable at home

While I work double shifts

To pay off last month's debt

Because I've lived through too much grief

To say goodbye to you

A moment / A whisper / A minute

Too soon

Rents due.

R/A

He invited me here on one of
Our first dates— I think I paid
(he was unemployed, you see)
And swears he used to help run
This Open Mic back in the day
If he is no longer welcome here
It is probably for the best
That man robbed me of the
Remaining innocence that I had
And belongs in a special cell
One with no windows so
He can grow to be as pale as
He prefers until he finally shrinks
Into the philosophical mind he
Longs for desperately and can
Finally, only harm himself.

NOBODY NEEDS TO KNOW

They likely wouldn't understand

"talk less and smile more"

Is a lesson I struggle to learn

Rather,

I prefer to hide my smile

In a mask

Along with my frown

Because the beautiful almond eyes given to me

By my ancestors

Keep the creepers at bay

Until I take my mask off

NOVOCAINE

My heart fell when you opted out
 of a drink at my place
You would rather ride the high of
 my good company and be sober with me
Now I'm not the sober one
 left to remember the whole story
 while the other half of that story
 gets lost to cross-faded memories—
Fantasies too good to remember, for you
And too hard to forget, for me.
You chose sobriety and my mind raced
 with the possibilities of how the night
should/could/would   carry on...
Never would I have guessed
Hours later, you'd wake the three of us up
With the roaring sound of your slumber.
My heart fell again when you
Politely ended the night
With two sleepy kisses
To wake me up long enough
To hear the door close behind you

If it wasn't for the outfit change, shedding off unnecessary layers
as we made our way to my bed, I wouldn't believe the night we had
Familiar and novel. Smiles and laughter. Keeping me grounded
My heart fell for you.

I shut down again— burnt out
 took 24 hours to process
The feeling of relief and elation
 I earned from your visit

.

.

.

I have been through so much already
 That when I made it home today
I just let out the most disconnected, airy sob

.

.

.

In my solitude, I cried for them
 the patients I said goodbye to today and
the families who blessed me with their trust

.

[Hold me | What is Love | I Was Never Poetic]

Our last hug felt like goodbye.

A door closing.

The end of an era.

Mourning.

Loss.

Regret.

I hate goodbyes.

Meanwhile

Your embrace felt like hope.

A possible new beginning.

Security?

It felt warm.

Made me feel wanted—

What will come of this?

SEASONS OF [LOVE] LIFE

He still has my heart

They still hold my attention

She lines my dreams with beautiful words

The others litter my fantasies with forgiving kisses

His absentminded B-O lingers on my pillow

Their cigarette scent lingers on my sheets

Her smile flashes behind my eyelids

The others keep me grounded under moonlight

His love healed me more than it hurt me

     And vice versa

Her love is a meek whisper of hope

Their love fuels me on dark days

They all have space in my broken heart ;

     They all fill the cracks in my armor

     They all manifest different versions of me

       All of them lost to the seasons

       My seasons of love.

Subjective

- **HISTORY**
- **BACKGROUND**
- **CONTEXT**
- **SETTING**
- **PERSPECTIVE**

ALL ALONE (REPRISE)

All Alone

On ly you he ar me

       I yell

No thi ng co mes out

       Am cold

Yo u ke pt me w arm

       I mi ss

Yo ur la ugh

Yo ur sm ile

Yo ur arm s

Wa nt to uch

          Cry so ft ly

          Cry lou dly

Cra wl in my sk in

We ep li ke a ch ild

          Abandoned

In t he ir cr ib

       I sing

For th e pr aise

       Of others

Yo u are t oo far go ne

LOVE IN PROGRESS

I & D quarreled for my attention

A_1 woke me with is kiss

K called me his dream girl

A_2 kissed me after church

N_1 Broke my heart first

J_2 stole my innocence

M gave me a fairytale love

J_3 brought me back to life

R helped me believe I was radiant

N proved me right

I am a collection of

Broken and restored women

A product of colonial religion

Laced with misogyny and

What's that word again—faith? hope?

For all of those I've loved before...

Take caution,

The future versions of self

Girls and Boys and others

Ready for love

Inevitably become victims

Of those pretending to be men

Desperate for love

In all the wrong places.

CLARITY

I'm not used to taking up space
I like being easy
To hide or
Be overlooked.
Especially in the front row
I can be missed. But
Now I have grown too much
Too much to be ignored.
Now I have grown too much to accept
Less than I deserve
Fuck being adaptable
I am accountable
and I must be
Regarded as such
I resent identifying with that label
My past selves wore with pride.
She was so sweet, so innocent
When she wanted to be.
She wanted to be

Perceived

But a professional manipulator
With no ill intent
Was her real disguise.

Striving to help others

Just to keep herself alive.

She tried to join them

But it wasn't the right time.

TU GRACIA ME ENCANTO

Autumn memories tainted by

My last Thanksgiving with

My family and

My first love.

Separate events, equally warm

In my heart.

His family

Saw me as his salvation

And mine knew

He was the death of me.

That perfect doll they

Dressed up in my youth

Should never be played with

By male clowns.

How could I choose such a fate?

Owlish he may be

But I loved that

Playing with him,

I finally felt free.

SKY FOREVER [A]MORE

1 – There is only one of you, so

2 – Let your dreams fly.

3 – Be fearless to keep your dreams alive.

4 – Be greedy for your ambitions

5 – Do not compromise nor settle on your dreams

6 – Fail. Fail. Fail again. And learn firsthand from these moments in time.

7 – Take risks // Be bold

8 – Surround yourself with the right people; find your community.

9 – Let others judge you // pay them no mind

10 – Don't take yourself so seriously

11 – Give back to those that accept your love

12 – never forget your roots

13 – Learn from your peers: the good, the bad, and the truths around you

14 – Ask questions, regardless of your confidence, it may save a life

15 – Make time for the people/places/things you love

16 – Honor music, art, cooking for the magic they hold

17 – You will not know everything; you are simply a student

18 – Make the most of all opportunities in your path

19 – Accept your limitations, and work with them

20 – Share your creations with those who are ready to receive these gifts

She's back and walking real slow
Hey I'm home--
Our song playing on low
Feels like the first time
So fly with me
So won't you fly with me
If it's you and me forever

Why don't you please dance with me

You and me right now, that'd be alright
If we chase the stars to lose our shadow
Peter Pan and Wendy turned out fine
So won't you fly with me
Fly... with me

You met at work, should've known better
Nobody's perfect, oh no

I'm not a saint, you've reminded me
I can't forget,
I won't forget
I don't regret it
We had fun, please don't forget me

Slowly now I see

You never listened to me

Remember this

I'm not just another victim

You won't forget

And I've already moved on.

MY DEAR JAMIE

For real, thank you for this

Can't begin to explain how much

This means to me

    So happy to experience a new city

        With you and

            Spend time with just us

    I miss you

And

    I can't wait to see you

I love you

    Hurry up and get here

NOTES TO SELF

I grew up fully immersed in the world

around me,

So much so,

It took me 23 years and

Relocating to the

other side of the country to see

How much I was missing

while already knowing too much?

DISNEY LESSONS

A dream is a wish your heart makes
When you're fast asleep
In dreams you lose your heartache
Whatever
You wish for it you keep [it in]
Don't speak them aloud or magic

will fade but share those dreams with us
the pool of hope restores power
But wishes ~~change/grow/evolve~~ might last the hour

And Not

      All Wishes

         Come True...

Villains know it best
We must live to work for that piece of extra special happiness
Marketed for children and princesses
The princes get theirs in the end
Onwards, go find your new dream
The time is near

Start with the face in the mirror

Start your journey alone

No matter how your heart is grieving

SEEN DECEMBER

You drew me as your faceless femme

Which hurt me because I

Worked real hard on my

Makeup and skincare

Slathered on snail glue

Followed by shark oil and

Carved out the hollows of my face

With copper and gold dustings

To finally be seen.

This was lost on you—

For the first time in my life,

Someone saw beneath my material mask

And drew my essence—

The picture that instilled

Rage, insecurity, contempt

Because *foolishly*

I drew offense to being

Depicted as your faceless woman.

UNREAD MESSAGES

Would you – just understand

Try to care and

Believe me when I say

I lived through your eyes

Admired you so much as a child

I lived through

Every heartbreak

                Every scolding

         Every judgement

                Every accomplishment

As your devoted admirer

All I wanted was the same from you

My blood sister

Why do I cry for you

When I am alone in my apartment

The one you never tried to visit

Another home away from home

Here I break my own heart

Yearning for your unconditional love

And I will die waiting for it

That is what I have learned

That is what I know now.

NO TITLE NECESSARY

One year ago, yesterday,
We purchased our last Christmas tree together
After skimming through more than one shop we
landed on the perfect tree

Even though you were getting annoyed
And the cost was more than we would have liked
It was the perfect tree for us
Perfectly imperfect

And the perfect tool to play dress up in a tangible sense
You allowed me the creative liberty I needed to heal
From the grief and lost feelings,
Feelings I buried deep in my bones
Unbeknownst to us
This was the last Christmas tree
You'll ever buy with me

This year I bought myself a plastic one and placed it on the shelf
Out of sight and out of mind to you
But a daily reminder to me
Of how inappropriate we are for one another.

Because yesterday I celebrated a new man's birthday
Between your eyes
And you didn't even notice.

PARTE DOS

I think you're jealous of me
I'm your second best
The second coming of you
The sequel that happened to be better than the original
Certainly more accomplished
Definitely gifted with a greater sense
Of humor and self

Something you helped me cultivate
Throughout our youthful years
Until life hardened you and
Glorified you for your beauty
Your fair skin and manageable hair
Tolerant of heat and manipulation
Not like my unruly and resistant curls

Your tempting shades of red
Stain pink on my olive skin
But your secondhand wardrobe fit
Like the hugs I grew to miss
Because you grew so thin
Your bones, a stranger in my arms
Holding up my best friend, no—
What was left of her memory

Forcing me to navigate this awkward era alone
Virtually alone in rooms full of shells
Time zones apart
Living opposite lives
Wishing for humanity
Seeking comfort
Settling for empty promises
Beautiful words with nothing between the lines
Clarity at last

The memories will suffice
My past-self depicted them more beautifully than the pictures in my hands.

TALE OF A DESPERATE LATINA: DESPERATE PLEA FOR HELP

Please, Listen—
Before impostor syndrome,
anxiety, depression, PTSD,
suicidal ideation,
and censorship bury us
next to him in the Land of the Free
when I want to be buried at home with
Brownie and Thomasa and their children
in the garden my grandparents planted for me
en la verdadera Isla del Encanto

Because we have been suffering in silence for too long
and people can't appreciate our beauty from afar anymore.

Because I learned from #Coco that #lallorona knew that
true love is worth fighting for.

And he knows that I am a girl worth fighting for
so he supports me in bed
[while I write to you in our bed, in our home that we have made in carajoland]

Because the home I was invited to six months ago was sickening.

BORICUA EN LA LUNA

They clipped my wings,

    Cut my fingers,

        Ripped off my mask,

                Taped my mouth shut,

      ...then worked me to the bone,

Walking on eggshells and then nails...

Forgetting that I have glasses to make sure I can see.

    Forgetting that I have a GPS to make sure I get home safe;

      One that I carry with me in my chest every day,

  so that I can phone home to *mi familia* and let them know that I am okay.

When I am too tired, I text,

    When I listen to *mi musica*

      I recharge enough of my battery

        I reconnect with whom I have lost.

Because no one can steal my voice and market it as their own while I still have both sides of my brain working on fumes 'til I can sleep peacefully in my bed.

    'cause I need to show these bible pushers that seeing is believing

   and the man they have been desperately seeking has been ME all along,

Because I inherited these **clase cojones** from mis Tios y mis Abuelos so that I could make it a safe place to come out of the closet and live the life we earned in paradise

      Here, while I am alive and well enough to do so.

HOW DO YOU EAT A MANGO?

1. I walk to my uncle's yard
2. Greet the turkeys that circle my feet with whistles and giggles
3. I wake up from my dream, craving the fruit of my lands
4. Muster up the courage to
5. Pick my keys up off the counter
6. Climb into my car, letting intuition guide me to the store
7. Sift through all the mangoes
8. Strange colors they carry but
9. The smell almost reminds me of home
10. Pick the ripest of the fruit
11. Pay my dues at the door
12. And when I arrive home
13. Struggle to peel the flesh with my hands
14. Sigh when no juices trickle down my wrists
15. Seeing the flesh buttery yellow when I craved sunset orange
16. I walk over to the blender and make a smoothie
17. To mask the taste of this foreign mango
18. With a frozen tropical blend and
19. Rum from home
20. To make the trip worth it.

IT CAUSES ME TO TREMBLE

Were you there when they tied him to the tree?
Who was there for me?

I was at your father's funeral
I was there for your dog's remission
I was there when you lost your precious purse
I was there when no one else showed up
I was there when your shoes broke, replaced them with mine

We were all there
Until my healing hands allowed me to see

I was there when my judgment was sullied
I was there when my honor was questioned
I was there when my heart ached over and over
   And again and again
I was there when you said I wasn't enough
   And yet, still, too much

I was there when you needed me
I was there when they tried to help
I was there when you said so
I was there when you said no

Until finally I am left alone...Give it time and I can realize
I am here to live, not just survive

Executive dysfunction takes over

Trauma response

I must escape to a safer place

Be honest with myself

I can love me more than you
And still show others their potential
For harm and good

Leave it up to them

I am here now, and then

I have enough love to give to you too.

My nature is to overcompensate—or overextend my kindness...

For ages the world demanded that I downplay my authenticity. With what seemed like minimal effort I lived gracefully. Or maybe it just feels like things transpired easily for me in the past. In truth, I was well adapted to working hard with little-to no rest nor reward.

I was always engaged in "activities." And when friendships were lacking, I still felt content, fulfilled by the relationships that lined those years of life. I miss that effortlessness of youth, that balance and harmony with societal expectations. For a brief period, I made me feel safe and at home in the world. Superficially, I had everything I needed and wanted... In retrospect, the lessons that bring me to this version of self are undeniably ratified with undertones clouded by melancholy.

Unconsciously, I am plagued by the blank spaces
in my life; equating them to micro doses of
failure disguised as rest. . .

Ultimately, it feels empty –lackluster // unappealing – and as much as
I don't want it to, the blank spaces and my awareness of them has also
assigned them to my character. As though with time, I have adopted these
adjectives as synonyms
for my personal attributes.

[{E M P T Y // L A C K – L U S T E R // U N A P P E A L I N G}]

I'VE LOST MY SENSE OF SELF SO MANY TIMES I'VE BEGUN TO
MIRROR OTHERS I MEET TO FEEL CONNECTED // TO GAIN
ENOUGH OF THEIR ATTENTION // TO NO LONGER FEEL LIKE AN
OUTSIDER. NO LONGER INVISIBLE WITH THE IMPOSSIBLE TALK
OF FILLING A 24HR DAY WITH PRODUCTIVE VS FULFILLING MO-
MENTS.

I yearn for the days when 18hrs passed in the blink of an eye and I felt like

I made a

difference

***

Now, I think back to my previous employments, mentally kicking myself for leaving certain spaces prematurely and abruptly, burning unnecessary bridges through my callousness, guided by ego.

In reflection, I can see the pain I hid and the burnout manifesting itself insidiously during that era of life. . .

I just wish I hadn't gone through so much alone // in solitude rather than in solidarity

I needed to thrive.

I am almost numb to failure / grief / loss

Almost.

RESPIRA REPRISE

Respira ondo

      Lo que sera, será

            Love is transient
                  Ever transforming –

                        Healing, never hurting

cursed   to   love   indefinitely
left   with   a   bleeding   heart
soiling   the   world   around   me
with   somber   poems   and   love-sick   notions
filled   with   empty   promises   to   myself
millions   of   letters   left   unopened
the   heart   of   a   child   with
dreams   of   becoming a   loving   mother
someday, cursed with a body that cannot sustain life beyond ordinary
means... loving me means accepting that I will
never   live   up   to   life's   expectations
so   I   make   up   for   it   in   gestures,
as   *grandiose*   or   *minute*   as   you   wish
for   my   greatest   failure   is
not   living   up   to   my   own   potential

SPEAKS ENGLISH // LOVES IN SPANISH

The heartache that accompanies

The somber tunes of adulthood

When you have finally moved away

From home to pursue the dream

Your community encouraged you to pursue

Now you must become accustomed to

Trade kisses and sideway hugs for handshakes,

Cold shoulders, and awkward elbow pats to avoid

Blames for crimes you have no intent

Of committing. . .

. . .crimes you have no intent of inciting. . .

Objective

- THESE ARE THE FACTS
- OUTLINED
- CAREFULLY DRAWN FROM LIFE
- DOCUMENTED
- EVIDENCE

I. *LATE BLOOMER*

Romanticizing long drives on

The highway from home to work

And from work to home

But when I catch sight of my angel numbers

Trios of 2s, 3s, 7s; then 6s and 9s

It is Game over

II. *LATE BLOOMER, IN BLOOM*

And then I snap back into reality

Finally allowing myself to feel

...grief

...anger

...happiness

Depends on the day

But usually,

All of the above

aka words men use to break hearts

...I'm sorry

...are you related?

...separate checks please.

...I lust you

...I appreciate you

...you're so pretty

...quit being/acting crazy

...ew, oh, my bad
(while hand grazes box of pantyliners in your car)

...Oh, not on your period

...I can crash here, right?

...I love you (in tears)

...you were my future

...I wanted a house with you

...I miss yew

...no we can't do long distance...

...too pretty or delicate to wear...

THE ART OF SADNESS

~~The~~ Saline from my tears ~~insidious water~~

Washes away my disingenuous

Mask of talc and pigment

~~The~~ Natural oils from my lids ~~impertinent fats~~

Lead the kohl to slip between

~~The~~ Fine lines of my smiling eyes ~~disconnected windows~~

Yearning to be liberated

From the toxins that

Help me feel human

2 hands wipe away the evidence

10 fingers massage away the tension

2 of 4 lips control the velocity of

Emotions spilling into the air

I have developed too many places to grab

May I just be held?

THEY SAY : 8.28.24

They say: to cut is to cure — cut that shit out — cut it off

      Time heals all wounds

      Treat others how you'd like to be treated

All bleeding stops eventually

But what if they have it all wrong?

      What if there's another, better, more appropriate way

      To navigate the hard times that are upon us?

What ifs were something I always avoided and yet

They seem to have a choke-hold on my journey

To new growth and opportunities,

When I used to say that

Everything happens for a reason

And now I desperately want, no, need that to be true—

Because all bleeding does stop eventually

TRIPLET POEM

The blood from my last patient was trapped under my fingers for 3 hand washes.

It took three tries before I realized my hands weren't clean enough.

She had a beautifully peaceful passing

And yet I couldn't let her go that easily.

I allowed myself [to hug her family] – vulnerability

Because I knew they needed it,

And I needed it too.

It took me three long-term relationships to realize I don't love men.

I don't love men who put me into a mold–

Either too rigid or too ambiguous,

And always too large in the wrong places.

The realization that I needed something more from love took 3 heartbreaks.

My parents finally had the son they wanted after three tries.

It took my mother three pregnancies to have the beautiful baby boy
my dad needed to quit smoking for good.

He set the standard for the ideal man growing up

He always sacrificed, when he could, to support his family.

Still, I find comfort in secondhand smoke.

It took my sister three tries to finally admit [smoking is a habit she can't quit]

But it didn't take me 3 tries to see the connection.

HAPPINESS ISN'T THAT HARD

I was so depressed on my 28th birthday

My partner of 4 years was unable to console me

I broke my own heart so many times over the last year

He couldn't find a way to break my depressive episode

With tickets to happiness

Instead, he tried to bring happiness to his bed

Where I was trapped in unspoken words

Of pain and betrayal

Which at the time

Said more about him as a lover

Than me as a partner

You see

I was mourning the loss of what I thought was my dream

Another job in California where I gave it my all

Only to last 95 days

Give or take a few

Primary complaint:

Too different

Too hard to control

Too inappropriate and inexperienced

Too quiet and too loud

Too detailed

Too slow

Too disorganized

Too exotic...

Reprimanded for being too much

and too little

And when I asked them to go find less

***

They obliged with telltale smiles and averted gazes

with perverted faces and

Whispers of obligatory pleasantries rushed me out the door

For being too much and never enough.

IT WASN'T ALL YELLOW

Yellow was my
First favorite color.
Neutral—
The color of sunshine.

As I grew up it became different shades of
Blue: turquoise, teal, ultramarine.
Colors associated with serenity and water,
Or plumes from exotic birds.
That gleam of blue off a Jay's wings,
Teasing you with their presence
That is my latest favorite color.

When I'm not lost in the spectrum of light
I look around and I see the rainbow around me.

Blues with purples and pinks,
Greens with yellows and reds,
Orange next to brown, then
Black with gold and sometimes silver.

...

What does this fascination with color say about me?

DISNEY ADULTS,

We have arrived to the era of Disney Adults

We have arrived to the era of Princesses and Villains ruling the Earth

Playing Judge and Executioner

According to the philosophies of thy holy Mickey

Mickey of the Mouse—
The Mouse who symbolizes the innocence of men
Yearning for love in childhood spaces

And in doing so, inspired generations of blood hungry Princes and Princesses

Desperate for happiness and now Our 21st century Heroes are actually the villains of your youth—

The 21st century villains are the poor unfortunate souls who hold empathy

For the weirdos and the misunderstood

We scorn the fools , Princes, and some paupers who dare to send

"you up" messages from bed while we dream of the cozy life

Only to wake up to never ending to-do lists for the modern adult

Past Due dates dancing on halos that we will inherit too soon

Because we learned to misplace trust on these fools—

Remember Selena / Whitney / Sister Sadie

All gone too soon

Thanks to the plight of success with

A little love on the side

* * *

The girl with the Miyazaki tattoo

Lacks in confidence

Creates in the dark to spare energy   Shows up every day

Resilience comes from hard times or   By any means necessary

La misma porqueria...

...hate the way they destroyed my innocence...

...referencing... the Dark I know well...

RUMOUR HAS IT

In your dreams you called me Paprika
In the waking hours you
Idolized every curve and scorned every rogue hair
But while you slept on me
I transformed into your favorite spice | sometimes sweet, sometimes hot
But smoked you hadn't tried in a while | maybe that's why
When she appeared in the light of day
I finally had the capacity and potential to get away

My preferred spice is cinnamon
~~[Which is clear to anyone who tries to get to know me]~~

Balanced and complimentary depending
On which version is available
You should have known that by the number of coffees
You supervised me making in my kitchen
Your perverted gaze disguised as admiration for my craft—
You must have been fantasizing about Paprika
But in my case it would have made a poor substitute

Rumour has it

In your dreams your sisters saved you from a mean girl
A crazy girl who tried to hurt you with her fists
Because her words went straight through you
In one ear and out the other
But while we stayed up all night
After tantalizing me with a nickname

Light-Skinned

I developed nothing but sympathy for the girl who took your love
Not for granted but by force and still had to fake it in the end

DULY NOTED

With all due respect

That is the respect

I determine you deserve

Te amo tanto
Pero no te quiero

Be still and know

That you may be

My first creator

Whilst I am

The final creator

~~Of my life, of my path//of my goals of my destiny~~

With all due respect

The responsibility to foster life

In this tortured vessel

Is more than a task

And I resolve to restore

Honor where you have failed,

Love where the failure was mine.

SCORPIO SEASON IS UPON US...

My precious feelings

They have finally returned to me

In shallow bursts that I welcome wholeheartedly

And fear when they shall leave me next...

May that time come long from now

For I have truly missed

The bliss of loving...

My heart stands heavy in my chest

| Beating }

                          | Still |

                                                  {Yearning |

...The bliss of loving with a magnetism blinded by the color red

The muse in Scorpio forces you to dig deeper

She is perceptive and creative, nay a soul seeker

They are soul readers gifted in Alchemy

Creating energy || Conceiving Life

through waves of wisdom she may grab you by the heart

until you feel everything and nothing

[~~centered on // curated for~~]

... her powers concentrated at targeted flesh,

...that with the most populous nerve bundles

No ill intent on her behalf, for patience is the most precious virtue

But for the poor unfortunate soul on her path:

Be ready or be destroyed   By your hidden truths

2024 MARCH 9

On this day, with 3 strangers

     I felt at home

     For the first time in years.

     At Eureka we shared

     Laughs and ate our fill—

     There was no pressure to drink,

     But my heart called for celebration

     I felt seen

     I felt wanted

Hindsight, this was the start of

One of my most painful heartbreaks

But this memory will not be tainted

Swept away by beautiful things

I speak as myself

I was among friends...

In just 3 months

Life changed completely

I am renewed...

Past midnight

     I imagine

How different

     Memories manifest.

CONFLICT RESOLUTION LOADING

Yesterday, I found his goodbye letters

2 for me

1 for his family

1 for the pets

1 for his friends

1 for everyone else

I read through them with tear-filled

Eyes glazed over with sorrow and fear

That I was too late – only to be reminded

Again, he is just a sad boy

In a simple man's body

I love him, but

I am so far out of love with the idea of him.

He is a friend on a good day, and

On days like yesterday,

We have history together.

***

My heart feels heavy

~~Like I anticipate something bad coming soon...~~

Anticipating the storm no one came prepared for...

I think the real feeling I have is

A combination of loneliness and anxiety–

~~I just masturbated to feel something different–~~

I pleasure myself in your empty bed just to feel something different

So, add a sprinkle of neurodivergence.

When I dig a little deeper

I know that I miss companionship

And fear that I'm going

To muck things up

By going too fast

Growing too attached

To feelings that don't fit

The situation, the person, the times.

I have not missed someone like this in a long time–

~~This saddens and scares me.~~ This sadness scares me...

Strikes me through the chest
Unable to hide the pain any longer...Seduces me to silence.

I would rather disappear at the moment,

And not have to wait to see how things transpire–

Live in unrequited love

To spare the feelings I've lost names for.

***

I feel empty now–

Reflection has allowed me

The pause I needed

And yet,

I still yearn to be blissfully in love with someone

To have them want to hold my hand;

Teach them how to make my body tremble– hell

I'd settle on receiving their beautiful smile

After sneaking a cheeky kiss onto their forehead.

I am hopeless

Destined to be loved or in love

Sometimes I can't tell the difference.

I crave the creativity to create something beautiful–

My brain ~~is~~ swollen with ideas

But my body is too tired to

Execute them alone.

***

I love independence and despise it...

I crave the companionship that comes with

Respect and adoration.

Can a cis-man pine for me the way I yearn for him?

~~I think not, or better yet, fuck the binary When~~

All I need is someone. I need someone

Who meets my wants and needs with

Genuine curiosity.

That should not be asking too much.

HOMESICK

*\\ can you miss a home that was never yours *
 // can it justify chasing the joy of youth //

Two weeks and counting and/but

I feel more lost than ever

Even hunger is lost on me

...and now

I direct my attention to the moon

How I envy her some days

I cried to her.

Danced with her.

Prayed for her.

And she will always be out of reach

Competing with the sun for my attention

But they'll never understand

They'll never know

I need them both to thrive

I need both of them to thrive

TOO MANY WORDS // TOO LITTLE // TOO LATE

It is nearly impossible

To sum it up

There is too much pain

Felt and never tended to

At least not by you

All of you failed me

Your hugs and cold shoulders

Trapped me in this box of

Self-deprecation // mania // depression

And doubt

Which I never deserved to live in

So please tell me why you find it so amusing

To push me down

Down past the dirt and water

To the center of fire

Where I was forged

Cementing

My fate

I MET GOD, ONLY FOR A MINUTE

When I met "God," his mouth moved but no words came out

Rather he spoke in the actions of others

Silently

Each word wrote them into existence

With judgmental glares

With knowing looks—

Looks that could kill

I knew it was Him by the phrases that filled

Pages of his prophetic book which

Perfectly imperfectly describes the human condition

Through the eyes of men and women

Who wouldn't be caught dead today

Speaking so freely about salvation and love

     For their neighbors

For their brothers and sisters

     For their parents

For their unrequited love(s).

No, today we shun those willfully ignorant every day:

Sacred pariahs pan-handling with words of peace and grace,

     Your shame on paper signs

Those humble servants speak His words into existence

     Proving how empty promises save no one

Proving how empty bottles save no one

     Proving how empty stomachs save no one

Proving how empty hands save no one

     Proving how empty pockets save no one

And we are all taught to preach the words that hurt
From people with seasons of guilt and shame
Parading themselves as forgiven
When we know damn well, they're the ones to blame
For the pain inflicted on themselves
And the pain reflected on others.

Holy father, mother, and spirit
Why must you hide between lines
Blurred out— an image of Christ
The one that doesn't look like me
But like all the men who failed me
Claims he took the L for me
When shit went down in his hometown
Claims he did it to protect me
A sacred act to be joined with his true father
Left his parents mourning for a son they never had time to love wholly
A son who never learned to be human, only holy
The demigod for Colonizer Religions
Capable of magic disguised as miracles;
Willing to teach but enlists others with no notes;
Longing for peace and finds it in the wrong places;
Capable of healing and reserves it for show;
Choosing to retreat because his Daddy told him so.

That mirage of man is worse than the first
He who stole sacred fruit to seduce his other half
Forcing her to bear more painful fruit
In labor and in spirit

Exiled for trying to resist temptation and failing

One chance was all they got

One chance was all it took

For that almighty god to scorn the first humans he swore to love

and you want me to think

the first time we met at those grand gates

that god would accept and welcome me

QUERIDA MIA

Tranquila, en paz— al fin estas solita pero nunca sola

De vez en cuando rezando a los Reyes Magos

Siempre pendiente de sus nietos

Yessenia, Adriana, Laura, Bryan, Ezra y Emma

Y la otra que está aislada en California.

No te preocupes por mi

A lo contrario

Me mandas bendiciones de lejitos

Sin decir que me amas, mejor aprecio todas tus acciones de amor

Preparando comida para los demás, eso es tu pasión

You see we exchange "bendiciones" as displays of affection

But our acts of love are prepared in food

Café con leche, calientito, y acabado de hacer

Color a mi piel— beautifully brown, mixed with a little cream

Preparado con un toquecito de azúcar, a mi gusto;

Pan de agua con un *chililín mas de mantequilla*

Y en otro plato, un huevito frito con jamón...

Para almuerzo, una empanadilla de pizza y uno de carne,

Del mejor quiosco al lado del puente, antes de llegar al hospital;

Nos sirven una coca cola y una cola champagne bien frio—

Y de noche, compartimos una botella de vino dulce y tinto

Cocinando arroz con gandules,

Con el sofrito que hiciste la semana pasada—

Dejandolo sofreír en la olla de aluminio con los

Cubitos de jamón, ajo picado, aceitunas rellenas, y hojas de laurel...

Mil olores, mis favoritos – ubicando a los vecinos por la ventana...

Y para el postre, nos vamos de viaje, a pie, al Baskin Robins
Los coquis contando los pasos hasta que llegamos
El timbre alerta el joven detrás del caunter— ya listos
Siempre pides lo mismo
Una pinta de chocolate para llevar...

La próxima vez que nos reunamos
Ya tendramos planes de olvidarnos del mundo arredor

All our troubles will be left stranded on the mainland

Para gozar cada momento de dulce compañía.
Por ahora hablamos por texto o por teléfono
Mensajes sencillos para aguantar las ganas.

I'm sorry... I love you—I hate you

Move in with me, please—save me

I'm lesbian for you—don't touch me

I'm hopeless and romantic—I'm scared

I fucked up—I'm so far from perfect

It hurts—I wish you could kiss me like that

I hate this version of me—you don't actually

Know me nor do I know you but I feel like

I've known and loved you forever; am I projecting?

Am I being annoying? Sorry my needs are many

I don't even want to share air with you rn

Am I a failure to anyone else? Be honest—

I want to meet you sober, and

Let you invite me over to meet your family—

I hope that kiss wasn't our last...

I'm sorry—I love you—I hate myself

I wish I hadn't learned so much yet

Still feel so fucking behind in life

You also tainted monogamist romance for me

With the love you're too afraid to give

Because you recognize it so well

That you [also]

Became acquainted

With the pain from

Having to lose it

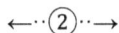

FIRE LEXICON

Word bucket | FIRE

*ember * burn * spark * ignite * kindle * fireball * stir * enliven * discharge * launch *
firebug * intense * radiate * light * bright * combust * flare *firetrap * firewater *
*fireweed * flame *love*

When issuing me a pet-name do not substitute mine with Love

Better yet, call me your Firebug

   Igniting our evenings with fireworks, invoking my preferred firewater
and I guess for you, Rosewood— unless

... Applewood is more to your liking...

   For I am the arsonist apt to set your soul alight

   With my radiant flame

Please, I plead with you

   Let me tend to your embers with sweet somethings

I know you cannot refuse

But you sure know how to put \\it// out — your cigarettes

Responsibly,

  handsomely,

    in any environment

If I could, let me place you, gingerly of course,

Below the mantle, but[t] safe in my arms

For I am fireproof— I can prove it

   But please don't ask to see my scars

Or you'll be disappointed that I hide them all too well

Assessment

- DIAGNOSIS
- INTERPRETATION
- PROFESSIONALISM IS KEY
- THE TRUTH CAN ALSO HIDE
- IN PLAIN LANGUAGE

HOW DO YOU IDENTIFY YOURSELF?

How do you redefine yourself?

~~Remove your identity from the one you have held onto for your whole life~~

Because the identity you ascribed to no longer serves you

And you have finally made peace within yourself

Enough to stop hiding from the labels placed onto you.

How do you identify yourself without too many labels

Labels that people will likely misconstrue... while also holding onto the pieces of you—

~~Deep down you know whats+'s true~~ ~~That you know as truth.~~

~~People are not labels~~

The ones you feel at your core and possibly have since birth...?

I think

These are the irrefutable parts of you

You know

The ones that your distant relatives have held onto

Between holidays and family trips home.

The parts of you that your guardian ~~reprimanded you for~~

Complimented or criticized in childhood.

The parts of you that allowed you to connect

Resonated with your closest friends.

The ones that you still love dearly as an adult, ~~if you are lucky.~~

The timeless parts of you.

What if...

Like the evolution of your favorite color

Or recently developed love for olives (which you had always detested)

These pieces of you can change?

Change comes with time,
And with...
Actionable items;
Active effort;
Applied potential;
Something driven by motivation...

What would it take for you to see and accept them?
What would it take for you to honor and tend to them?
What would it take for these changes to blossom?
So they can live boldly in your core—
So that even your distant relatives can see them—
And even you can wear them with pride...
These identifiers are yours
To manifest and to love,
So that others can have the chance to love them too.

FEED THE BEGGAR WITH YOUR WORDS

Material things can have monetary value
As living things can have
Spiritual and Emotional value

We are allowed to take up space
Privileged in fact
We are to take up Space

Whereas robbing others of their energy is a crime against humanity.

TO FEEL WHOLE AGAIN

I've had this poem stuck in my head for some time now
Mulling over it because I just can't find the right words
In English
To convey the feelings
I know too much and too little about

           I'm not used to taking up space
           I've learned not to take up space
        Been led to believe that it is wrong to take up space
Stay a size less than 10, but less than 5 is best.
Earlier this year I finally fit a size 6,
        And now I'm starting to grow out of them...
        And the feeling is anything but positive...
        And now I hate myself for growing up...

Until I get to unbutton those pants
At the end of a meal
Sat in the driver's seat—

As soon as I walk through the front door
Of my home...apartment.
Yeah, I know that home should be in me.
And that I should be my home.
But this year I've lost knowledge and
Developed insecurities,
Cemented my trust issues,

And constructed elaborate mazes to avoid connection with others

Except for one or two people — y cuidao.

I revealed my truest self to one person this year

And it destroyed me 3 months later.

That's the danger of falling in love with an artist.

Two artists involved in a spring love affair

And they'll always be

fighting for the role as the

Art or the Artist.

And if they're a photographer or philosopher— run away.

Two months later and I had another man in my bed.

One day later I vowed

To be the only one I entertain in my bed.

Because I'm allowed to take up SPACE —

As much space as I need

As much space as I damned-well please.

As much space as I need to feel whole again.

ENTERTAINMENT IS A SCAM

The content we receive from our handy media devices

Are a reflection of where we are as a society.

Think about it.

If they produce and release a piece of work that does poorly—

No one would watch, and many lives would be negatively affected.

But who decides what content is ready to be received by the public?

Our founding fathers, of course.

They blanket the world with a shroud of confident goodwill;

Ignorant of the "unintended" negative consequences of their actions

Producing generations of confounding variables and outcomes

Tasking our mothers are with cleaning up the aftermath:

Dealing with the consequences.

They are dealers of consequence, exercising the resolve to create change whereas hereditary concerns are outside of their scope of practice.

And when I say we and our,

I am referring to the mothers of the world, and her people too

Independent of faith, ethnicity, size, shape, or color.

~~For a moment, reflect on the tropes and stereotypes that have been passed down generation to generation, like in the cases of our blondes:~~

~~Evolved to shine with their stupidly honest personality in spite of the neurologic or cardiac issues formatted into their~~ DNA—

[the genetic makeup we cannot wash nor excuse away]

But they will try.

Just like our factual history.

You can cover it up and dress it anyway you want;

And still the truth will make itself known.

In   time   we   evolve   to   change   our   world

To change our world

In calculated doses

Determined by humans that are no longer with us on Earth.

Their reign is more cumbersome,

Insidious even,

Because although they meant well

They're the reasons we're so fucked.

Point mutants occurring with each day, month, year — generating

Generations of offspring with differences

Attributed to just a few base pair switches.

Chromosomal hybridization: a presumably *random* outcome of

Genotypes and phenotypes.

But can this be true?

Dig deeper. Think bigger.

The Gods, emperors and Kings,

Perceived higher powers

Beyond reach

Have created Anonymous Decisions on your lifeline.

Before and after your lifetime

And they couldn't possibly know of the countless varieties

Of outcomes TNTC, Too Numerous to Count

Just like the number of suffering individuals on this earth.

We are not free, until we are all free.

We are not free, until we are all free.

#free Gaza/Palestine

#free Sudan

#free Congo

#free Puerto Rico

#free child laborers

#fuckice

#nokings

BORROWED FROM ANOTHER TIME

I am a collection of stories
I am a collection of stories that
Make up all parts of me.
Hidden from the world
The moment comes where
Hiding from loved ones feels like
A betrayal to myself

Finally, I see

Life has been filled with shame and doubt
Like I was always playing a role
Rather than being my authentic self.

As I've gotten older, I've found that
Wisdom deep inside
Connecting parts of me that were hidden
Inside of loved ones
Deep inside, I hide
My incomplete stories
Their hidden meanings even I can't find

Until this story is done being written

I must hide these truths

   For love

    With love

               Sincerely,

                 me

LO SIENTO

Mi querido viejo, lo siento.
Mi ángel de la guardia
((Amargó compañía))
No me desampares...

Descansa y deja descansar.
Por favor
Te lo juro que te amo tanto
Pero tranquilo—
Descansa por favor.

Ya entiendo el ritmo Borinqueño:
El ritmo de tu tierna corazón
Roto y lleno de amor
Un amor antiguo
Para la llorona
Mi querida viejita
Que te amaba a su manera
Pero ya

Déjala en paz.
Ella no te hace falta.
Déjala vivir y disfrutar la vida que le queda.
Te lo juro, te amo tanto
Pero ya no me haces falta.
Querido viejito y veterano,
Descansa en paz.

SHUT UP AND LISTEN

I talk to myself

Because

I know I am strong enough to handle

This kind of love

Too tough for men

And too passionate for women

I talk to myself

To fill my ears

Take up space

So the demons stay in my past

And I remain free in the future

I talk to myself

Because

I am allowed to interrupt myself

And still get my point across

I talk to myself

To keep me from hurting others

So their view of me is pure bullshit

But we can sleep peacefully knowing

I am strong enough to manage

I talk to myself

So one day I can hear the pain and know that I deserve better

PANDORA'S BOX

Lo Siento, esto era mi regalo.

Lamentablemente, con esto me jodieron la vida

Y dañaron la sorpresa por la última vez.

Los amo mucho pero sus sentimientos me valen un pedo y medio

Aquí te regalo la otra mitad.

I'm not proud of what I did.

I'm not sorry that I did it—

I am sorry it took me this long.

I am sorry you still don't understand why I choose to be selfish—

Porque me sale de los clase cojones

Que me regalaron antes de nacer.

Passed down from generations

Of tolerant women

Forced to raise men they didn't birth

And women they wish they didn't have to.

Estoy que no aguanto mas

Lamento que nunca me van a entender

Ayunque ya me perdonaron

Superficialmente, como antes,

Pero no por siempre.

Hasta aquí llega.

Si tu Dios quire.

My pen has all but dried out

The reservoir for love

More than half empty

All that is left is

The love reserved for me.

When you finally miss me

You can find my love in:
unread messages,
handwritten notes
scattered around the donation piles,
next to photographs of our past selves
Ph[r]ases you borrowed from me and shared with
Friends I delivered to you

All the pieces of me scattered

Expertly so

One day I may be

Made whole again

Unfortunately for you

That is no longer a dream of mine

I love this shallow person I've become --

Less room to grow, yet

More considerate of the marks I make

I DON'T HAVE A FAST CAR

I find solace in long drives—car rides

Alone in the car

Just me and the music / carrying me through traffic /

Along with the wind through the clear sails around me

Crashing against my curls like waves

No, like butterfly punches

Try as they might, they cannot hurt me

Land on my ears

But

The music has already taken their rightful place

On my heart

So that my brain can repent and reflect

Till my heart is content

And finally accept—

I need to stop running away,

From home,

Pretending it resides by the waters

On this foreign coast

That would swallow me whole

The next time I let its waters

Bring me down

To your level.

Time to leave

These poor unfortunate souls

Behind.

INFP (IDEALISTIC NURTURING FOOL IN PERSPECTIVE)

Do you ever have this unshakable feeling

That you need to cry—

A deep, guttural, heart wrenching cry

So that your child self can rip out of your chest and

Spill into the tears that paint your face

Like this invisible external pressure

From the week or the world

Has all gotten to be too heavy,
like Gravity was God and He chose you as their unwilling prophet,

Instilling in you their worst punishment for keeping yourself grounded.

Weighing on you while you're down—

This unbearable weight on your shoulders

Bearing down on your spine and your hips

Such that all your space is reduced to nuisance

<u>Crying for the pain / Crying in vain / Crying for some semblance of relief</u>—

Maybe all you get is release

From that added pressure you put on yourself

For years—decades even...

It isn't just me, right? Don't you wish it could stop?

For there to be a better solution

A resolution from

The pain // The grief // The regret

In the end, that would be enough

But only in the end...

#POESIA

I need time

      To miss you

      To tidy up my space

      To recharge my social and

      Emotional batteries and

To feel like myself again.

I need space

      To grow and heal

      To be loud and quiet

      To miss you and

To find myself again.

I need music // sound // art

      To focus on the present

      To appreciate life

      To articulate feelings

The not so pretty ones

That I lack vocabulary

                  To express in words, you understand

                  So, you can validate the feelings

                  and I can finally find

                  Peace in my heart

SIMPLY QUASI

You are deformed by your lived-in experiences.

You are ugly by the way

The hands who raised you in a toxic bubble

Taught you to react to circumstance with fear and aggression.

Lack of accountability has transformed you

Into a grotesque version of the man I knew,

Highlighted by the nightmares you confessed to me—

Visions of what our future would have been

Until I drew the boundaries in our lives,

Removing the veil only strangers cast to

Liberate me from that toxic macho vice.

You call me worse names than ugly while I feel

Fully free, capable of accepting and welcoming

The masculine energy inside me that

Always scares weak men away.

You destroyed the appeal for lust.

One look,

Two cups of tea,

Three nights playing house, and

Another three months of pretending,

Just to grow tired of the charade.

Finally

Realizing you bore your talons into me

Slowly and reassuringly

Because that is what broken women are used to

First you grazed my neck with your nails

Next you caressed my collar bones and hip bones,

Clawed through to my love handles

Latched on from behind so I couldn't see it

But just like I can feel your macho gaze on my ass and tits

I could feel you carve yourself into me.

I used to think I deserved this love

That maybe I could save us both from it

Because you taught me how to handle micro doses of pain

More palatable than the lectures of layers of *torture* applied to you

In your past life which left *you* broken beyond reproach

At last,

I consent to sever all ties,

Amputate each limb you

Infected with your

Toxic legacy

WORKING DOG

Obsessed with work

Unable to rest because

I can't stand this pace

I prefer to live on 1.5x speed

Or more at all times

Because I'm more

      productive

          needed

               appreciated

In that same little window of time

I can candle so much more

And when I've spent almost all of my energy

I finally used the smallest morsel

To tend to myself

Treat myself to the most profound sleep

Laced with vivid dreams

To get through the next day

QUASIMODO—REDEFINED

You are deformed by your lived-in experiences.

You are ugly by the way—
the way the hands who raised you in a toxic bubble taught you to react to
circumstance with fear and aggression.

You are ugly by the way—
the way lack of accountability has transformed you into a grotesque
version of the man I knew.

...bruised and scarred with a strong ass back to carry the burden you claim
to own

...permanently disfigured by the oppressors you wish nothing but harm on

...harrowing presence distorted by the lessons you wear tattooed on your
flesh.

You are ugly by the way—
the way your voice aims to comfort but gets caught in a fabricated stutter
forced by that reflexive response you learned to feign ignorance— excuse
me, *innocence* around
ignorant minds that sympathetically stroke your ego.

My memories of you are highlighted by the nightmares you confessed to me,

Visions of what our future would have been // could have been until
I drew the boundaries. Removed the veil only strangers cast to
liberate me from that toxic macho vice.

You call me worse names than ugly while I feel fully free,
more capable of love by accepting and welcoming
the masculine energy inside of me that always scares weak men away.

~~You destroyed the appeal for lust disguised as carefree love.~~

I loved you recklessly—

One look,
Two cups of tea,
Three nights playing house, and

Another three months of pretending, just

To grow tired of the charade.

Finally,

I realize you bore your talons into me

Slowly and reassuringly

~~Because that is what broken women are used to~~

First you grazed my neck with your nails,

Next you caressed my collar bones and hip bones,

Clawed through to my love handles

Latched on from behind so I couldn't see, But

Just like I can feel your macho gaze grab hold of my breasts

I could feel you carve yourself into me.

Because that is what broken women are used to.

I used to think I deserved this love.

That maybe I could save us both from it,

Because you taught me how to handle micro-doses of pain

More palatable than the lectures of layers, such torture applied onto you

In your past life which left you

Broken beyond reproach.

At last,

I consent to sever all ties, deliberately

amputate each limb you infected with your toxic legacy...

The circumstances where I let you into my dark places

serve me as a permanent reminder of your deficiency as a man,

more monster than human,

disabled only by your mind.

MY STYLE IS...

My style is journalistic and raw:

Streamlined thought between day/ze of controlled chaos.

My style is sensitive and callous:

Loving in Spanish but my words come out in English.

My style is literal and symbolic:

A garden that I tend to when the plants are / dying, decayed, dead /

My style is Perceptive and Introspective:

Unable to mask the reality I live in while

the one I accept heals and haunts me.

My style is lost and seeking:

Hoping to find the words that form from music
In my head as I take control of
The soundtrack to life
Privy only to my ears

Until others can open their eyes to this
beautiful melody

Created romantically and scientifically

In my style. . .

UNEMPLOYMENT IS HERE FOR YOU NOW

I am over and under qualified for every job

        I pray it does not reflect my inadequacies over my achievements

How about neither? Because

        Today I choose to call out the institutions that failed me

        By paving the way to this career

        Only to struggle to get a part time job on the weekends

Well below my pay grade

        So that I can rest my overachieving mind and still manage to

Pay my bills on time... you see I'm a self-sufficient doctor

And company(s) don't promote self-sufficient people – at least not without the stipulation for fair pay and fair treatment as a minimum requirement you must downgrade yourself for this job.

Like I said, I'm a self-sufficient doctor.
First pick of the litter of Interns, and first to be fired too.

Because the racist cucks who ran the practice

Valued my doctorate as a token of diversity for tolerance of adversity

Glazed over the fact that I survived "Zoom University"

Informed by unique lived in experiences plus extra curriculars in combat, creative writing, and

Microdosing greens enough to stay
mentally, physically, and emotionally fit

Until the impostor monster made an ass of you and me.

Slurring my English with medical jargon and Spanish anecdotes

Made me the perfect candidate

To push perfectionism like a miracle supplement

Washed down with programmed professionalism

Down my throat

Only to see it come back up through my mouth and nose

Grateful it spared my eyes and brain

Four months of this mysterious disease and

Finally, we had enough of the charade. . .

The time for judgment right around the corner

Being called to that dreadful room where

Four paired eyes were already in attendance

Gleaming to see through the mask

[Adorning thy lying face]

The red flags are laid out on the table

Ready to call out the perfectly timed excuses — professional lies

Postponed this meeting too many times

Too many times to talk your way outta this one

Unemployment is here for you now

I AM

Alondra : an extinct brown songbird from the island of Puerto Rico
better known as Borikén // Borinquen

I am a connoisseur of art
But I prefer to hide behind instruments and canvas
Until now
Rather recently, I learned the power of my voice
My memories
My unique lived experiences
That connect me to fellow tortured souls—
Empaths and omniverts/ambiverts
Mi gente empática, queer, and marginalized:
 latiné and Hispanic and mixed
The ethnically ambiguous that hail from remote Island paradise but
are expected to wear the American flag with pride
That flag that no longer resonates with me
La bandera puertorriqueña es la mía
De la verdadera Isla del Encanto
Que tantos buscan y nunca lo pueden ver:

Los flamboyanes que amo tanto

Y los coquis que me lloran

El güiro que me llena el alma
Al lado de los tambores y los jíbaros

Jamás lo puedes imaginar

     Lo mucho que extraño mi isla...

     Esta cañón que

          lo tengo que describir en Spanglish

               y que todavía no me entienden...

RESUELVE // AFIRMA

I have lost so much
For the privilege of
Practicing medicine in
The USA.

The trouble I find is
I live in English and
I love in Spanish.
My palate may be
Too spicy
Too quiet
Too honest
To be sustainable.
And yet,
I have so much love in my life.

Some may say I am truly blessed
To always be loved
      Yet rarely understood
      is the cross that I never asked to bear.
And the sacrifice I make
      to find peace within,
      to share my light with the world.

TODAY I CHOOSE TO BE FREE

They promised us a lemon tree

I waited for two years

But it never grew

I asked him where the seed what planted

And his response struck a dismal chord

Scanning the yard for signs of growth for days, then weeks

Until it dawned of me...

He thought I was the garden

The one we didn't need after all

This time I'll choose a guava tree and a coconut palm

And he can buy all the fruit he prefers

Each to our liking.

~~Together~~

~~Or rather~~

~~Apart~~

There is love in compromise, but when the love has gone sour
And the compromise is both self-serving and self-limiting
Can you still call that love?

Today I chose to be free

Like the little brown songbird

Free of ignorance

And of blame

I'm sorry Peter can't apocalypse right now

I'm not sorry for him, I'm sorry for me/us/we— as in:

We could use a homie/handyman to help carry

This weight that:

        1.   We never asked for
        2.   We never consented to
        3.   We never x y x . . .

While he's over there drinking tea with his lucky lady lover

Sus Primas Hermanas are drinking coke or double shot espressos

Over whatever medium helps us throw them back

       // Suck them down // Swallow them up//

     Fuck Ice, leche, cristal   Prefiero azúcar, sal, o miel

Leaving the salt of the Earth   behind us for
you (all) to remember us

By the way it permeates the pores of your skins
Assaulting your wounds while soiling the folds / seams / crevices of
            your car / your couch / your throne

While we pray that

          ...our journeys to and from Hell and Earth have earned us
enough

Karma that one day our

 ...souls may rest

                if not in this life,

                   ...then hopefully the next

IN STILLNESS WE RISE

No energy left to see through glasses...   Stillness | stagnant silence

No room to raise   Associated with being alone

my arms in   Left alone to my devices

A language of visual symbols   Stillness becomes my enemy

Only those disabled can see   Time to spend more money

Use me   Fighting the need for R & R

Putting up [with] prose and con artist lists

All I have left is this pen and pad—my plume is lost again

          No energy left to send a message for

Help!

          Deciding between wants and needs

There is not enough   Like they aren't all valid

Energy to make you   Like they aren't of equal importance

Want to see me   Process / Reflect / Repeat
          Process \ Reflect \ Repeat

Wrap your arms around me   The cycles of shame to fill my time

One more time   With stolen minutes of past phases

No energy left to   Dreams converted to nightmares

Feed the lie   Driven by lack of securities – collateral damage

You [n]ever cared for me   Damned if I do Damned if I don't

This cursed body   Ask for your hand when

You resented this unstable mind Your arms were crowded then

Cradled around your knees, a natural position I wish was foreign to me,
but you were not my first saviour and yours was not the first

Life I saved but the last I needed to

Mine was the last I wanted to

Plan

- ACTION
- COMMANDS
- DEMANDS
- RECOMMENDATIONS
- CLOSURE

LET ME BEGIN AGAIN

I'm sorry that I yelled the last time we were together

The thought of losing you consumed me so much that I let rage win—

Let me begin again.

I'm sorry that I asked you to commit to me too soon

Bared my soul to you and let you see the worst version of me

When you were stuck in a honeymoon daze—

Let me begin again.

I hate that our last kiss was the most beautiful

One we shared and you were too hurt to enjoy it

                                    too hurt to hold me

I hate that you knew it'd be the last time—

Let me begin again.

I hate myself more than I hate you—

Let me begin again

I'm sorry for blaming myself and expecting you

to know enough to save me too—

Let me begin again…

Hi. It has been a while /huh?/ can we [just talk]?

LISTEN/OYE COVER (SPANGLISH DREAMGIRL)

Listen, tengo algo que decir, no puedo ya seguir pensando en ti

Oye, mmmh como *grita mi canción*—préstale atención, ¿puedes oír?

Hoy no sé quién soy, ni se adónde voy

Olvidarte hoy es mi misión – de tu prisión, quiero estar, ¡libre-e-e!

¡Oye! —esto no tiene salida, ya nada sirve que digas

Tengo q escapar lejos de tu hogar, es mi misión

> *Oh, buscare mi propria luz—no seas insensible*
>
> Soy más de lo que fui por ti; Llena de valor—voy a seguir.

Yo tengo q encontrar mi vo-o-o-o-oz...

Nunca quisistes...que me fuera a volar...

Tallar mi identidad, que gran error... Hoy grito: ¡*No quiero más calor*!

Liberarme hoy es mi lesión. ¡De tu sudor, por fin estoy libre!

¡Oye! —esto no tiene salida, ya nada sirve que di-gas

Tengo q escapar lejos de tu hogar, fue mi misión

> *Hoy, buscare mi propria luz— yo soy la más sensible*
>
> *Soy más de lo que fui por ti; llena de valor al fin estoy feliz...*
>
> *Tengo que liberar mi voz—*

"Yo soy/fui tu gran creación" por eso es que me vo-o-oy

¡Dime Adiós, Ciao mi amor!

Listen! To the song here in my heart, a melody I start and here, I comple-e-ete!

Oh, Tengo aquí mi propia luz, yo soy la más sensible.

> *Soy más de lo que fui por ti; llena de valor al fin estoy feliz.*
>
> ¡Tuve que encontrar [Aquí yo encontré] *mi voz // my voice*!

I.   Boys will be boys

It's the entitlement for me

It's the fact you thought *that* poem was about you

when I haven't seen you in years

As I'm about to tell you that my ex of eight years is back in my DMs asking

"Can we be Civil"

When we don't even talk

When he didn't even try to say hello first

When we don't even live on the same coast

And you really thought that poem was about you

When you let him break me into a million pieces over the course of 3 years

So that you could put me back together

When we only shared one kiss under the stars

And he still has the ring I never even saw...

Yeah sure, not all men are bad

But every good boy does fine in my book

Until I'm the one crying alone

While his scent haunts my pillows

While his voice taints my radio

While his words hurt my brain

While my heart rebuilds itself

Again

II.   Therapy Queen // Tuesday, April 18, 2023

I am ugly

And I am proud

Because that first line

Is a lie that I will

No longer tell myself.

My beauty resonates from within

Everyday

Whether I see it or not

That is up to me

I am beautiful

Inside and out.

III.   Time to retire him

My 2015 Hyundai Accent

Rolls of my tongue like an inside joke between friends
The homie was my ride or die
Literally
My noble steed who got me
From Orlando to Pomona
Safely
With the little I could fit from my childhood bedroom
To live out my childhood dream
Of becoming "La Doctora favorita de la famlia"

That bittersweet dream
Well, sweet dreams turned bitter by the
Culture shock of Los Angeles
I met them, los "Angeles"
Ally, Haley, Andrea
Mis Angeles
The ones de la Guardia I used to pray for
Kristen, Shadi, Gina
The ones that stabbed me in the back
The ones who turned their backs
When I needed them most
Ally, Haley, Andrea
But this poem isn't about them

This poem is about my moving castle
My 2015 Hyundai Accent

He was a gift from my father,
The perfect companion
His seats molded to my figure
The radio dials just my arm length away so I could
Scan through stations with the gentle turn of my fingers
The steering wheel worn on the right-hand side
Because I would rest my left arm on the window
To catch my head on tired drives
Tracing the lanes from town to town in the IE

Searching for a static home
A fantasy that he refused to lead me to...

***

I wish I didn't trade him in so soon
10 years was not enough
To make peace with losing my childhood home
And my innocence.

LAMENTATIONS OF A MODERN SHE/THEY
IN AMERICA

Born on an island, that feels far, far away
Further and further from the top of my priority list
With each passing day on the mainland...

My biggest lesson so far is that:
Money is not a renewable resource.
At best you can burn money when the power is out
And you need to keep warm,
But in this economy, where trees are few and far between
On this stolen land that was run by them
You dissociate by hyper-fixating on details.

The trouble with supply and demand:
Capitalism lands you in an inverse relationship
With happiness and joy on the other side too.
Whereas things made by hands or with hands and other things,
They have a tendency to produce a parallel relationship—
Unless perpendicular is more your style.
You see with goods, the goal is pleasure or satisfaction in some regard
But I have plenty of things in mind that I'd give you a
Fair trade for...if you're good for it

The trouble is the year is 2024 and
The Cheetolord Supreme has been elected president [again]
And I feel homesick in my own home
While we work our asses off trying to pay past due bills

Joking about splitting the rent

When you can't even hold my hand in public.

Lord forgive my quick, short-tempered heart

But how can you let this happen in the Land of the Free

          Haven't we done enough

      Haven't we cried enough

          Haven't we prayed enough

Haven't we sacrificed enough

      Haven't we died enough

At least we live up to the title "Home of the Brave"

Riddle me this Lord,

When we stood each morning as children

One hand on our hearts to sing our nation's song

Were you listening, Lord?

And then was it you or someone else who accepted

This to be our fate?

MISS ME WITH THAT:

You're an inspiration! You **strong** *lady*—
You're one cool dude, man...

Wait.
I like that one, kind of
Almost as much as I detest
Being likened to a *lady*

Call me Doctor Strange
Call me queer
NO— don't give me that look
I thought I was an inspiration
In your eyes
I thought I was, strong, so strong
In your eyes
I can't be all of the above.

Maybe in Spanish: mirame y escuchame
Gusten y vean
Lo que sera, será
Que Dios me Bendiga, ¿verdad?
Sin ninguna duda
Que Dios me iluminé, ¿verdad?
Aquí estoy iluminando mi vida
Con la luz de La Madre de Dios
Con la luz de la Diosa que me dio

Vida y Libertad

Bueno, aquí estoy llena de luz y amor
Listo para regalárselo a todo el mundo.

Pero primero que nadie, ese amor puro, me toca a mi
Solamente a mi

UNTITILED (2)

Being Defensive was Taboo
Became Offensive to teach you a lesson

                        Aggressive / Profane / Vulgar

In calculated doses
To match your toxic masculinity
A frail sense of security
Which you failed to deliver
Nor could you save me from
My perceived feminine urges
While my needs became more preventable

                        Buried / Dissociated / Hidden

By the grace of doctors
Smarter than yourself
I was freed from the madness
I had tolerated for years

A POEM FOR GAZA

My favorite olives are the ones

I've never tasted

The ones that refuse to grow on

Sullied soil

Mixed with native blood

Sweat and tears

From their loved ones

Learning to replace dinner with sleep

Breakfast with panic attacks

And lunch with picture-perfect grief

MISS ME WITH THAT (REPRISE)

Me thinks you need to update your perspective when it comes to me
You see
Pushing negativity and intentions where they are not meant to be
Especially negative intentions on my words
When I obliged to provide *solicited* advice
That is the greatest sin a friend can do to me

Me thinks you need to work on yourself a little more
Before you try to expand on our relationship
This ship that has sailed many a times
And yet, Always finds a way home

Me thinks you're ready for deeper reflection
Self-Attention
To cure your self-mutilating behaviors
That you honor
That you hold onto
That you can't get enough of
That you believe to be the right way to exist

Me thinks I'm done being hurt by you
 Anthropomorphizing your self-inflicted insecurities—Ideologies
 Personified self-image that don't really align with your higher purpose

Me thinks I'm done pacifying your ego
That shameless foe, laced with woes
Has driven a wedge between us

Far too many times

Me thinks we're both ready for love
Not with each other
That has already been deeply rooted and well established
But love in its purest form
Platonic and familial – the love that we strive for
The love that's been broken too many times

Me thinks you're scared
Scared of tapping into that capacity that you hold
So near and dear
Close to your core
That you hide it from everyone with layers
Upon layers upon layers upon
Layers and layers of boundaries
Rewritten as insecurities
Blaming hypersensitivity
When really
It's time
For you to
Just be

I WON'T SAY IT

I curse the fates for time blindness
They deliver you to me
At the best and worst times

Clad only in loungewear and moonlight
We talk the night away, walk the night away
You with the hair that matches my eyes
Gifted me my first fiery wings
I steal glimpses of eyes I could swim in
A confusing blue that I know
Are no good for me
Lest I admit to losing
This game of
Platonic intimacy

If only I had stars for hair to guide me through this
Dreadful feeling
My perfect companion
Is not dead, but hung up on a
Beautiful someone
While I entertain their friend— Nay Perfect Companion
Reminiscent of the man I loved
Fated to be fucked, married, killed by the curse, that is My Love.
The only exception is, all I wanted was you.

WHEN I DIE

Bury me in Linen
Or another compostable fiber
I don't give a fuck which
But please bury me at the base of a willow tree

After my funeral
Shave my hair off and
Braid it with the swinging branches
Of my willow tree
Let her hold space for me
Among her roots and arms
As I give her the nutrients she needs
To provide solitude and comfort
For the other lost boys and girls
That question her gravidity and wisdom

Let her teach them
Or better yet show them how
To learn / To feel / To accept love in life,
And
To learn to let go.

DEAR ANGEL OF MUSIC,

Angel of Music
Sleep,
I love you

What is this strange feeling?

Angel of Music
Wait,
I beg you

Stay by my side, guide me

Angel of Music
Fuck,
I hate you,

Why do you speak freely?

ODE TO THE SUN

You tell me good morning, despite my mood,

  You see on days I feel blue

You give me space behind transparent/temporary barriers

  Giving me hope that when the mood passes

I have something beautiful to look forward to.

  When the day comes to a near end you have this

Unique way of checking in -- drawing attention to yourself

  In the most curious way

Sometimes bold, sometimes muted

  Always ambient, never subtle

Keeping me grounded in your presence when I give myself the time

Thank you for being one of the few constants in my life

Thank you for being a beacon of hope

  Even on the darkest of days, I know

You're only a few hours away...

  How do you instill balance in our daily lives?

One day I hope to learn

  For now, I promise,

On days that I have the energy

  In the morning, I will salute you with a choreographed piece

To bask in your warming words – gentle and bright

Disguised as light

To carry me through another day

TO THE VETERINARY CLASS OF 20-SOMETHING

Hold space for empathy

Offer that freely to your past, present, and future selves.

So that you may never feel like your cup is less than full.

Do not forget : medicine is an art

To err may be human

But first you must strive to do no harm

Do not forget : this is a career

You were called to this role

But this role is not your life

I encourage you to remember the words in our oath

The oath that you will likely forget the lines of

as summer comes and goes,

But in time you will remember

the words, the phrases, the intentions

Imbued and amended in three stanzas

To recognize that our duty is to advocate health *and* wellness

Prioritize welfare with each life we serve

Perfect our craft to prevent suffering when we can ;

And relieve the pain that comes with time.

Recall the words written through collaborative effort by our colleagues and

Predecessors as powerful reminders for why you answered the call

I hope you never lose yourself to the field, nor

To the pressure of employers, peers, clients

I hope you make the time to look inward

Find your compassion and practice with a kind heart

To produce work you can always be proud of.

Please remember:

    Where you started

    Who you sought comfort from on your worst days

    When fear almost robbed you of your dream

    What experience drove you to apply for this seat

    Why you deserve to be referred to as Doctor

[Again]

Hold space for empathy

Offer that freely to your past, present, and future selves.

So that you may never feel like your cup is less than full.

Look around, from the stage to the seats around you are

Rows of colleagues // competent human primates

that have sworn the same oath

With a promise to being lifelong learners,

Stewards of scientific knowledge,

Committed to medical advancement and public health.

Do not forget : medicine is an art which we practice

Now is not the time for the Renaissance of Perfection.

Now is the Era of Creative Healers.

GRIEVE ;

Nature doesn't ask for attention.

When you open your heart to it

Beauty surrounds you, calls to you.

When you open your heart to it,

Creatures of all shapes and sizes can find refuge in its chambers

And dance with your heart strings.

For when their hearts have arrested,

Once more their souls can find refuge in yours.

Through the cracks that only nature can fill.

Give it time.

10.22.2024

I have her hands

Los de Mamá

Te lo agradezco tanto

Por elegir

Escoger amor

Y familia

Y tu carrera

GRATITUDE

Start Slowly | Play often | Love unabashedly | Take caution
Love carefully | Ponder Life
       Use   childlike   amazement
       Borrow   elderly   reserve
Love yourself | Dance freely | Honor the seasons | Instill Balance
       Seek harmony
Find community
       Foster humility
Find humanity
       Love others
End shame

HARMONY

You loved fully
Lost everything
And survived

Don't you dare
Believe
You are anything but
Resilient

LEARNING TO LOVE MYSELF AGAIN

Finding comfort in cracked heels

Keeping me grounded as they grate

Against each other–

Wearing loose clothing that caresses

My curves, my arms, and

Bulbous bikini lines...

I wish my curves weren't concentrated near my center

Though I welcome this shapely,

Feminine build I've grown into.

The soft folds behind my ribs

A hidden gift from the mother who passed them onto me.

The gentle movement of my flesh coated wings when I agitate my arms...

Arms that carry extra room so that I may evoke the warmest hugs at a moment's notice

The silent squeak of my hips, my thighs as

They strike one another between steps, uniquely mine.

These are the many ways my body

takes up space

      keeps me protected

When my thoughts and prose

      Keep me small and less than kind.

UNCENSOR ME

I am a violent person
With
Gentle tendencies–
In action I aim to cause
No harm
Simply
Let my words

Slit your wrists for you ;
Tie you up and hold your attention
While I trail deliberate
Kisses down your neck to
Your vulnerable inner thighs
Tease your anxieties out with my
Tantalizing tongue–
Trailing back, back to your ears

So hopefully
You can see
How sweetly
I keep you alive
To torture you
With implied consent
Just the way you like,
You like it that way,
You taught me that way–
Sweet love of mine

We won't get caught this time

In the lie of love

Fueled by night

Gone by daylight

So we can play pretend

Like my memory

Some made up fantasy

Of you and me

Fueled by jealousy and

Centuries-old pain

Sweet love of mine.

Let the shame

Hide behind your dark smiles,

Moans and Cries

Transform them into

Your heart's desires

The ones you don't speak aloud

Because we don't

Kink shame here.

Sweet love of mine.

Let me be your shelter

Alondra (she/they), nicknamed "Bird" in grad school,is an artist, poet, and scientist.

Their first love was animals, which is why most of her life was dedicated to the dream of becoming a veterinarian. This "friendly neighborhood Dogtor" usually spends their free time watching movies, painting, or vibing to music (when they aren't doom scrolling or reading or writing). Recently, she has put her dreams of becoming an Avian Specialist (yes, Bird Doctor) on hold, to heal and return to her second love—art. At (more than one) "rock bottom" returning to writing helped offer the perspective needed to thrive in the real world. Seemingly, the dynamic nature of poetry allowed them to romanticize life's struggles in a therapeutic way.

Through creative works, Alondra hopes to share her light with others to rekindle that spark seemingly lost to time.

Alondra (el/ella), llamada "Bird" por sus colegas de la Universidad, es artista y poeta ademas de ser un científico.

Su primer amor fueron los animales, por eso dedico la mayoría de su vida logrando su sueño de ser veterinario. Esta "Dogtora" prefiere pasar el tiempo viendo películas, creando pinturas, o gozando música de varios estilos (cuando no esta "escrolleando" por los redes sociales ni leyendo o escribiendo). Recientemente, pospuso su sueño de ser especialista en aves (sí, doctor de aves) para recobrarse y volver a su segundo amor— el arte. En sus momentos más bajos, escribir le brindó la perspectiva necesaria para prosperar en el mundo real. De nuevo descubrió que el dinamismo de la poesía le permitió romantizar las dificultades de la vida en una manera más terapéutica.

A través de su creatividad, Alondra espera compartir su luz con los demás con la intención de reanimar esa chispa de amor por el arte que se sentia perdido al tiempo.

Publishers Note

Daxson publishing was created to help marginalized artists publish their work, so the world can hear their voice. The vision for this publishing house is to help people get their work out there, and not have them struggle finding their way through the publishing process. Everyone's voice deserves to be heard, and we are here to help. If you are interested in submitting a manuscript, email daxsonpublishing@gmail.com.

Support our cause by buying books from daxsonpublishing.com.

www.ingramcontent.com/pod-product-compliance
Lightning Source LLC
Chambersburg PA
CBHW071151120626
46546CB00006B/2221